John Malam

523 273 66 8

First published in 2012 by Wayland
This edition published in 2016

Text copyright © John Malam

Wayland, an imprint of
Hachette Children's Group
Part of Hodder & Stoughton
Carmelite House
50 Victoria Embankment
London EC4Y 0DZ

Senior Editor: Joyce Bentley
Designer: Elaine Wilkinson
Picture Research: Shelley Noronha

Dewey number: 941'.085'092-dc23
ISBN: 978 0 7502 9878 0

10 9 8 7 6 5 4 3 2 1

Printed in China

An Hachette UK company
www.hachette.co.uk
www.hachettechildrens.co.uk

To find out about the author, visit his website:
www.johnmalam.co.uk

Picture credits
The author and publisher would like to thank the
following agencies and people for allowing these pictures
to be reproduced:
All graphic elements: Shutterstock. Reginald Davis/Rex
Features; front cover: Topham Picturepoint; back cover:
The Print Collector/HIP/TopFoto; p1: Shutterstock:
p2: Stamps, John Malam; p3: Rex Features; p4: Topham
Picturepoint; p5: TopFoto; p6: The Print Collector/Hip/
TopFoto; p7: John Malam; pp8-9: Everett Collection/Rex
Features; p10: TopFoto; P11: Topham Picturepoint; p12-16:
Daily Mail/Rex Features; p17: Rex Features; p18: Reginald
Davis/Rex Features; p19: PA Photos/TopFoto; p20:
PA Photos/TopFoto; p21.

Contents

1926 BIRTH OF A PRINCESS

*I*n the early hours of Wednesday 21 April, 1926, a baby girl was born at 17 Bruton Street, London. This was a special baby, born into the British Royal Family, and from the moment of her birth she was a princess.

The baby girl was born with blue eyes and fair hair, and she was her parents' first child. They were Albert and Elizabeth, the Duke and Duchess of York. Albert, whom everyone in the family called 'Bertie', was the second son of King George V.

In Windsor Castle, 23 miles to the west of London, King George and Queen Mary were fast asleep – but they had left instructions to be woken as soon as there was any news. At four o'clock in the morning they were told about their new granddaughter. Later that day, they drove to London. People cheered as their car motored along Bruton Street and came to a stop outside number 17.

The first photograph of Princess Elizabeth, taken just a few days after she was born.

On 29 May, 1926, five weeks after her birth, the princess was christened at Buckingham Palace, the Royal Family's home in London. As her forehead was touched with holy water from the River Jordan, in present-day Israel, she was given the names Elizabeth Alexandra Mary.

Royal Custom

Royal christening gown

At her christening, Princess Elizabeth wore a gown made from white satin and fine lace. The gown was 85 years old, and had been made for the christening of Queen Victoria's first child in 1841. Every royal baby has worn the same gown at their christening since then.

Princess Elizabeth with her parents on her christening day, wearing the Royal christening gown.

THE LITTLE PRINCESSES

*W*hen Princess Elizabeth was a year old, the family moved to a new house at 145 Piccadilly, London. It was a big house with servants, quite close to Buckingham Palace, and this is where the Princess spent much of her childhood. On the top floor was the nursery where she slept and played, and where nannies looked after her.

Princess Margaret (left) and Princess Elizabeth (right).

As she learned to speak, the Princess found it hard to say her first name. Instead of saying 'E-liz-a-beth', she said 'Lillie-beth'. Her grandfather, King George, liked this very much, and he began to call her 'Lilibet'. The name stuck, and from then on she was known as Lilibet to everyone in the Royal Family.

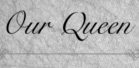

Our Queen

Still Lilibet today

Queen Elizabeth has never grown out of her childhood name of Lilibet. To this day, on Christmas cards she sends to her family, she signs herself 'Lilibet'. It's a private name, used only for the closest members of the Royal Family.

Princess Elizabeth had a younger sister. She was Margaret Rose, born in 1930. At first, she was going to be called Ann Margaret, but her grandfather, King George, didn't like the name Ann, so it was changed to Rose, which became her second name. From about the age of six, a governess, Miss Marion Crawford (known as Crawfie), gave Princess Elizabeth her school lessons at home. Once a week a music teacher taught her to play the piano. She enjoyed her piano lessons, but didn't like all the practice she had to do!

Cousins came round for tea and games, there were pillow fights at bedtime, and lots of fun and laughter. It must have seemed a wonderful childhood for the little princess, but as she approached her tenth birthday, her whole world changed.

The little princesses, Elizabeth aged 6 (left) and Margaret aged 2 (right).

1936 YEAR OF THREE KINGS

*I*n January 1936, King George V died. His body was taken to the Houses of Parliament, London, and for five days, thousands of people walked past his coffin, in silence. Princess Elizabeth, aged nine-and-three-quarters, was taken to see her grandfather's lying-in-state. As she came before the coffin she saw four men standing at each corner. They were the dead king's sons — her father, Albert, and her uncles David, Henry and George.

King George V, Princess Elizabeth's grandfather.

As King George's first son, David was next in line to the throne. This meant that when King George died, David became the new king. However, instead of becoming King David, he wanted to be known as Edward, which was another of his names. He became King Edward VIII.

King Edward VIII, the first son of George V and Princess Elizabeth's uncle.

Within a few months, King Edward wanted to marry a divorced woman, but the British government said he could not do this and remain king. So, in December 1936, King Edward abdicated – he stopped being king in order to marry the woman he loved.

Our Queen

Next in line

Princess Elizabeth was next in line because she was older than her sister, Margaret. But, under the old rule, if her parents went on to have a son, he would have been next in line, not Princess Elizabeth. This rule changed in 2011 to make it fairer to girls. In future it will simply be the first born child who is next in line.

Next in line was King George's second son, Albert. He became the third king of 1936. Instead of King Albert, he picked another of his names, George, and he became King George VI. From the moment her father became king, Princess Elizabeth was then next in line to the throne.

What the monarch's numerals mean.

I = 1st II = 2nd III = 3rd IV = 4th
V = 5th VI = 6th VII = 7th VIII = 8th
IX = 9th X = 10th

King George VI, the second son of George V and Princess Elizabeth's father.

LIFE IN THE PALACE

*I*n February 1937, the Royal Family moved into the most famous house in the world — Buckingham Palace. Princess Elizabeth had a nursery with its own bedroom, and nearby was a nursery and bedroom for Princess Margaret. School lessons carried on much as before, but Princess Elizabeth still had to be in bed by 7.15pm.

Buckingham Palace must have seemed like an adventure playground to the little princess. It had long corridors and hundreds of rooms, and when she was exploring with her governess, Miss Crawford, Princess Elizabeth said she needed a bicycle to travel around on! The gardens were equally big, and ducks nested along the banks of the pond. One day, when the Princess was looking for a nest, she slipped and fell into the water, and ended up covered in green slime. Miss Crawford sneaked her back into the palace and cleaned her up before anyone found out what had happened.

Princess Elizabeth as a Girl Guide, aged 17. She is about to release a carrier pigeon with a message to Chief Guide Lady Olave Baden-Powell.

The Royal Family at the coronation of King George VI. Princess Elizabeth and Princess Margaret are in front of their parents (King George and Queen Elizabeth) and grandmother (Queen Mary, to the left of King George VI).

Our Queen

At her father's coronation

Princess Elizabeth's father was crowned King George VI on 12 May 1937. She was so excited she was awake at five o'clock in the morning. At the ceremony, she wore her first long dress, a cloak, and silver-coloured sandals. On her head was a small crown called a coronet, which had been made specially for her.

When Princess Elizabeth was 11, she became a Girl Guide in the 1st Buckingham Palace Guide Company. There were 34 girls in the Company. The older girls were Guides, and the younger ones, including Princess Margaret, were Brownies. Meetings were held once a week in the summer house, in the garden of Buckingham Palace. The Princess enjoyed the meetings because she could make friends with girls her own age. It was a happy time for her, but it was not to last. In 1939, World War II began, and the 1st Buckingham Palace Guide Company was closed down.

1939-1945
PRINCESS AT WAR

Princess Elizabeth changing the wheel on an army lorry. Her army number was 230873 which she remembers to this day.

Princess Elizabeth was 13 years old when World War II began in 1939. It was a frightening time when bombs were dropped on Britain's towns and cities by German aircraft. Buildings were destroyed, and thousands of men, women and children lost their lives.

The Royal Family was in danger if they stayed in London, which was a target for the German bombers. For their safety, the family was moved to a secret location.

It was Windsor Castle, a fortress a few miles to the west of London, where they were guarded by soldiers. Every day, King George VI drove to Buckingham Palace for meetings with the Prime Minister and other important people, before returning to Windsor Castle at night.

Our Queen

Speaking to children everywhere

On 13 October 1940, Princess Elizabeth broadcast on a BBC children's radio programme worldwide. She was 14 years old.

'I can truthfully say to you all that we children at home are full of cheerfulness and courage. We are trying to do all we can to help our gallant sailors, soldiers and airmen, and we are trying, too, to bear our own share of the danger and sadness of war. We know, every one of us, that in the end all will be well.'

As Princess Elizabeth grew older, she urged her parents to let her join the army. So, in 1944, when she was 18, she joined the Auxiliary Territorial Service (ATS). She wore an army uniform, drove trucks and learned how to look after their engines.

Then, in May 1945, Germany surrendered. The war was over, and celebrations were held across Britain. In London, Princess Elizabeth and her sister slipped quietly out of Buckingham Palace, and the teenage girls mixed with the joyful crowds on the city's streets. No-one suspected who they were.

Princess Elizabeth's parents, King George VI (in uniform) and Queen Elizabeth, inspecting bomb damage at Buckingham Palace in 1940.

1947 THE ROYAL WEDDING

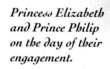

*S*hortly before World War II began, Princess Elizabeth went with her parents and sister on a cruise along the south coast of England. They sailed to Dartmouth, in Devon, where the Royal Navy had a college that trained young men to be officers. The Royal Family went ashore and were shown around the Royal Naval College.

Princess Elizabeth and Prince Philip on the day of their engagement.

Our Queen

Wedding dress

Princess Elizabeth wore an ivory silk wedding dress made from material from her family as well as donations of brocade and silk. It was decorated with 10,000 pearls. Nylon stockings were hard to find after the war, but Elizabeth was sent hundreds of pairs from well-wishers when her wedding was announced.

Princess Elizabeth was 13 and during her visit she was introduced to Prince Philip of Greece. He was 18, and was studying at the college. Miss Crawford, Princess Elizabeth's governess, later said the Princess 'never took her eyes off him the whole time'.

The Princess and the Prince became friends. They wrote letters to each other throughout the war, and Prince Philip visited the Royal Family at Windsor Castle.

In 1947, they became engaged, and on 20 November that year were married at Westminster Abbey, London. Princess Elizabeth was 21. More than 2,000 guests came to the wedding, and the happy couple were showered with 2,500 wedding presents. Princess Margaret gave them a picnic hamper, and Miss Julie Alloro, a four-year-old girl from Brooklyn, USA, sent a turkey – and a note asking for the wishbone to be sent back!

The wedding of Princess Elizabeth and Prince Philip. Princess Margaret (next to Prince Philip) was chief bridesmaid.

Royal Custom

Wedding ring of Welsh gold

Princess Elizabeth's wedding ring was made from a nugget of gold mined in Wales. Gold from the same nugget was used to make six royal wedding rings between the years 1923 and 2011. There is not enough left to make any more rings from it.

1952 ELIZABETH BECOMES QUEEN

In 1951, King George VI became very ill. Although he seemed to get better, his doctors feared he did not have long to live. That October, Princess Elizabeth and Prince Philip visited Canada and the United States of America in his place.

They returned, and then a few weeks later, on the last day of January 1952, Princess Elizabeth and Prince Philip went off on their travels once again, this time to Kenya, East Africa.

On the night of 6 February 1952, King George VI died in his sleep. Far away in Kenya, Princess Elizabeth was at Treetops Hotel – a famous hotel built into the tops of giant trees. As she watched elephants and rhinoceroses drinking at a waterhole beneath the treehouse hotel, she had no idea that her father had died and that she had become Queen.

Arriving home in Britain as Queen Elizabeth II. She was met at the airport by Prime Minister Winston Churchill.

Royal Custom

Accession Day of Queen Elizabeth

Queen Elizabeth II became queen on 6 February 1952. It is known as Accession Day – the day she acceded or took over as monarch.

It was several hours before she found out. A message was passed to Prince Philip, and he broke the news to her. The next day, she flew home to Britain, wearing the black clothes that she had packed to wear in the event of her father's death. She had left Britain as Princess Elizabeth, but returned as Queen Elizabeth II. She was 25 years old.

The lying-in-state of the body of King George VI. More than 300,000 people filed past the King's coffin.

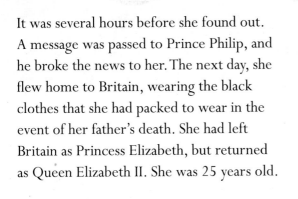

1953 CROWNING THE QUEEN

Queen Elizabeth II was crowned Queen on 2 June 1953. The date was picked because weather forecasters said it was usually a sunny day, but they got it wrong — it rained. Coronation Day was a holiday, and schools and workplaces across Britain were closed. People held street parties, crowded around tiny televisions to watch the ceremony in black and white, or they listened on their radios. In London, three million people lined the streets.

The coronation of Queen Elizabeth II. She is dressed in her coronation gown and wears St Edward's Crown (the coronation crown).

The coronation was at Westminster Abbey, London. At eleven o'clock, the Gold State Coach, pulled from Buckingham Palace by eight horses, drew up outside, and the Queen stepped out. She walked slowly down the aisle and sat upon King Edward's Chair, used at every coronation since 1308. A white tunic was draped over her shoulders, then a golden one, and finally a heavy robe woven with gold thread.

Our Queen

Longest reign

On 9 September 2015, Queen Elizabeth II became the longest reigning monarch in British history, taking the record from her great-great-grandmother, Queen Victoria. On that day, she had reigned for 63 years and 216 days.

She was presented with mysterious objects, each one a sign that she, and she alone, was Queen. The Orb, the Sceptre, and the Rod were placed into her hands, and the Coronation Ring was slipped onto the fourth finger of her right hand.

Finally, the most significant moment arrived, as the Archbishop of Canterbury lowered St Edward's Crown onto her head. The congregation called out 'God save the Queen!', the Abbey bells rang and guns fired salutes all over London.

The new queen leaves Westminster Abbey in the Gold State Coach. This coach has been used at every coronation since 1821.

Royal Custom

Coronation crown

The Crown of England is St Edward's Crown. It is only used at a coronation ceremony, and was first worn by King Charles II at his coronation in 1661. It is made from gold and is covered with diamonds, sapphires, emeralds, rubies and pearls.

ROYAL DUTIES

Queen Elizabeth spends most of her year at work, even when she is on holiday. There are just two days a year when she does not work — Christmas Day and Easter Sunday.

Once a week the Queen has a private meeting at Buckingham Palace with the Prime Minister, or they talk on the phone. They talk about what's happening in Britain and the rest of the world.

The Queen cutting a ribbon in 2010 to mark the opening of the British Garden in New York City, USA.

Every day the Queen receives 200–300 letters. Many of them are invitations. Members of the Queen's staff decide which ones she should accept. A timetable is then drawn up for the Queen's schedule. Throughout the year the Queen attends hundreds of official engagements. She visits places in Britain and around the world, attends opening ceremonies of new buildings and events, and holds meetings, lunches, banquets and Garden Parties.

The Queen holds four Garden Parties a year — three at Buckingham Palace and one at the Palace of Holyroodhouse, Edinburgh. About 8,000 members of the general public are invited to each Garden Party, and a lucky few actually meet the Queen. Cups of tea, sandwiches and slices of cake are served to the guests.

ROYAL EVENTS

State Opening of Parliament

Each November, the Queen attends the State Opening of Parliament. It marks the start of a new year in the life of the British government. The Queen enters the House of Lords wearing fine robes and a crown, then sits upon a golden throne. She reads out a speech which has been written for her, describing what the government plans to do in the year ahead.

Remembrance Sunday

On the second Sunday in November, the Queen, the Royal Family, the Prime Minister and members of the army, navy and air force gather at the Cenotaph, London. At 11 o'clock, Big Ben strikes, and everyone stands in silence for two minutes. When the silence ends, the Queen places a wreath of red poppies at the Cenotaph. This solemn ceremony remembers all those who have died in wars and conflicts since World War I (1914-18).

Investitures

Several times a year, ordinary people are invited to meet the Queen at an investiture ceremony. They have done good work and the Queen recognises that by giving them special medals called honours, such as an MBE (Member of the British Empire) or an OBE (Order of the British Empire). A man can be knighted to become a Sir while a woman becomes a Dame.

THE ROYAL FAMILY TREE

KEY

―――― Line of succession

 Monarch

r. Years of monarch's reign

Queen Victoria
1819–1901
r. 1837–1901

 King Edward VII
1841–1910
r. 1901–1910

 King George V
1865–1936
r. 1910–1936

 King Edward VIII
1894–1972
r. 1936

**Prince Charles
Prince of Wales**
1948–

**Princess Anne
Princess Royal**
1950–

**Prince William
Duke of Cambridge**
1982–

**Prince Harry
of Wales**
1984–

Peter Phillips
1977–

Zara Phillips
1981–

**Prince George
of Cambridge**
2013–

**Princess Charlotte
of Cambridge**
2015–

**Savannah
Phillips**
2010–

Isla Phillips
2012–

**Mia Grace
Tindall**
2014–

Next in line to the throne

1. Prince Charles
2. Prince William
3. Prince George
4. Princess Charlotte
5. Prince Harry
6. Prince Andrew
7. Princess Beatrice
8. Princess Eugenie
9. Prince Edward
10. James, Viscount Severn
11. Lady Louise Mountbatten-Windsor
12. Princess Anne
13. Peter Phillips
14. Savannah Phillips

King George VI
1895–1952
r. 1936–1952

Queen Elizabeth II
1926–
r. 1952–

Princess Margaret Rose
1930–2002

Prince Andrew
Duke of York
1960–

Prince Edward
Earl of Wessex
1964–

Princess Beatrice
of York
1988–

Princess Eugenie
of York
1990–

Lady Louise
Mountbatten-
Windsor
2003–

James, Viscount
Severn
2007–

23

YEAR-BY-YEAR

1926	Age 0	Birth of Princess Elizabeth
1930	Age 4	Birth of her sister, Princess Margaret Rose
1936	Age 10	Her father becomes King George VI; she is next in line to the throne
1939	Age 13	She meets Prince Philip
1940	Age 14	She sends a radio message to the children of Britain in World War II
1942	Age 16	Her first public engagement when she inspects a regiment of soldiers
1944	Age 18	She joins the Auxiliary Territorial Service
1947	Age 21	She marries Prince Philip
1948	Age 22	Birth of Prince Charles, her first child
1950	Age 24	Birth of Princess Anne, her second child
1952	Age 25	King George VI dies; she becomes Queen Elizabeth II; she moves into Buckingham Palace
1953	Age 27	Her coronation, in Westminster Abbey
1957	Age 31	She makes her first television Christmas broadcast
1960	Age 33	Birth of Prince Andrew, her third child
1964	Age 37	Birth of Prince Edward, her fourth child
1977	Age 50	She celebrates her Silver Jubilee (25 years as Queen); she becomes a grandmother
1993	Age 67	Buckingham Palace opens to the public
1997	Age 71	She celebrates her Golden Wedding (married for 50 years)
2002	Age 75	She celebrates her Golden Jubilee (50 years as Queen)
2007	Age 81	She celebrates her Diamond Wedding (married for 60 years)
2010	Age 84	She becomes a great-grandmother
2012	Age 85	She celebrates her Diamond Jubilee (60 years as Queen)
2015	Age 89	She becomes Britain's longest reigning monarch (63 years 7 months)

GLOSSARY

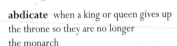

abdicate when a king or queen gives up the throne so they are no longer the monarch

accession when a person becomes the new king or queen, he or she accedes to the throne

banquet a large meal with many courses

coronation a ceremony at which a crown is placed on the head of a new king or queen

coronet a small crown

divorced when a man or woman stops being married and becomes a single, unmarried person once again

fortress a building which is defended by strong walls, such as a castle

governess a woman who works for a family; her job is to teach the family's children

House a group of kings and queens who belong to the same family; the present Royal Family is the House of Windsor

investiture a ceremony at which a person is invested or given an award or honour

lady-in-waiting a woman who attends to the Queen

lying-in-state when the body of a dead monarch, leader or politician lies in a public place for a few days for people to visit and pay their last respects

monarch a king or queen

next in line the next person waiting to be king or queen

Orb a hollow gold ball covered in jewels; it represents the Earth, and the monarch's role as head of the Church of England

reign the period in which a king or queen rules

Rod a gold staff with a white dove at one end; it represents the monarch's powers of fairness and mercy

Royal Standard the personal flag of the monarch

Sceptre a gold staff or rod with a massive diamond at one end and a gold cross; it represents the monarch's life on Earth before God

throne a special chair on which a king or queen sits

Windsor this has been the surname of the British Royal Family since 1917